EXPLORING THE WORLD

MAGELLAN

Ferdinand Magellan and the First
Trip Around the World

BY MICHAEL BURGAN

Content Adviser: Professor Sherry L. Field, Department of Social Science Education,
College of Education, The University of Georgia

Reading Adviser: Dr. Linda D. Labbo, Department of Reading Education,
College of Education, The University of Georgia

COMPASS POINT BOOKS
MINNEAPOLIS, MINNESOTA

Compass Point Books
3109 West 50th Street, #115
Minneapolis, MN 55410

Visit Compass Point Books on the Internet at *www.compasspointbooks.com* or
e-mail your request to *custserv@compasspointbooks.com*

Photographs ©: North Wind Picture Archives, cover, back cover, 1, 2, 4, 6, 9,
10 (top), 11, 12 (top), 13, 16, 24, 25, 26, 29, 33, 35, 37, 38 (bottom), 39, 40, 44; Visual
Language Library, cover (background); Hulton Getty/Archive Photos, 5, 12 (bottom); 18 (top
and bottom), 28; XNR Productions, Inc., 7; Stock Montage, 8, 10 (bottom), 14, 27, 30, 38
(top), 46–47; David Lees/Corbis, 15; Corbis, 17; Don Fawcett/Visuals Unlimited, 19; M.
Timothy O'Keef/Bruce Coleman, Inc., 20; Beth Davidow/Visuals Unlimited, 21; Frank
Krahmer/Bruce Coleman, Inc., 23; Charles W. McRae/Visuals Unlimited, 31; Max & Bea
Hunn/Visuals Unlimited, 32; Peter French/Bruce Coleman, Inc., 34; Tony Arruza/Corbis, 36;
Preston J. Garrison/Visuals Unlimited, 41.

Editors: E. Russell Primm, Emily J. Dolbear, and Melissa McDaniel
Photo Researcher: Svetlana Zhurkina
Photo Selector: Catherine Neitge
Designer: The Design Lab

Library of Congress Cataloging-in-Publication Data
  Burgan, Michael.
  Ferdinand Magellan and the first trip around the world / by Michael Burgan.
    p. cm. — (Exploring the world)
  ISBN 0-7565-0125-3 (hardcover)
  ISBN 0-7565-1146-1 (softcover)
    1. Magalhaes, Fernao de, d. 1521—Journeys—Juvenile literature. 2. Explorers—
Portugal—Biography—Juvenile literature. 3. Voyages around the world—Juvenile literature.
[1. Magellan, Ferdinand, d. 1521 2. Explorers. 3. Voyages around the world.] I. Title. II.
Series.
  G286.M2 B87 2001
  910'.92—dc21   2001001510

Copyright © 2002 by Compass Point Books

Printed in the United States of America.

Table of Contents

A Bold Voyage

The sun had not yet risen in Sanlucar de Barrameda, Spain, on September 20, 1519, as Ferdinand Magellan prepared to sail for Asia. On board his five ships were about 250 sailors

Magellan's ships

Chinese pepper merchants

and enough supplies to last two years. The ships also carried bells, jewelry, cloth, and other items Magellan could trade for spices when he reached his **destination.**

At this time, Portugal bought and sold most of the spices that reached Europe. Portuguese ships traveled eastward, to India and trading ports in Asia. Some of the spices came from a chain of islands in the South Pacific Ocean known as the Moluccas, or the Spice Islands. The Portuguese returned to Europe with pepper, nutmeg, and other valuable spices.

Magellan took a bold, new route to the Spice Islands. He sailed west, not east. The trip he began in 1519 took almost three years and only one of his five ships finished the voyage. That vessel and

The Spice Islands as shown in a nineteenth century engraving

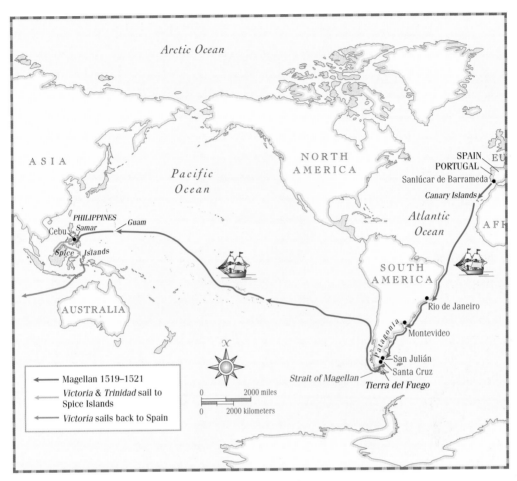

A map of Magellan's voyage

its eighteen sailors completed the first known **circumnavigation,** or circling of the globe by water. Sadly, Magellan did not survive the trip—he died in 1521 in what is now the Philippines. But he won lasting fame for planning and leading one of the world's great voyages.

An Age of Exploration

Ferdinand Magellan was born between 1470 and 1480 in northwest Portugal, perhaps near the city of Porto. His name in Portuguese was Fernão de Magalhães. Magellan was a member of the Portuguese **nobility,** so he had the rare **privilege** of studying at the king's court, though his family was not particularly wealthy or powerful. He learned math and other skills that later helped him as an explorer.

Portugal's royal family had helped start a great era of exploration. Using only sailing ships, the Portuguese traveled to Africa

Ferdinand Magellan

and Asia. Other European kings also sent sea captains to search the world for lands they could claim for their kingdoms. The explorers took gold and other treasures back to their homelands.

Portugal's neighbor, Spain, also joined the hunt for riches. In 1492, Spanish ships led by Christopher Columbus sailed westward in search of a new sea route to Asia. Columbus believed he had found this route. Over time, however, other explorers realized that Columbus had not reached Asia. Instead, he had found the Americas, lands few Europeans even knew existed. Both Spain and Portugal sent ships to **investigate** this new world.

A fifteenth century ship called a caravel

Magellan was one of the explorers who believed these lands lay between Europe and Asia. Ships could sail west and reach Asia—if they could get around the land that blocked their path. Magellan thought

Columbus reported to the Spanish court after his return from the Americas.

he could find a **strait**, or sea passage, that cut through the Americas to another ocean. In 1513, the explorer Vasco Núñez de Balboa had become the first European to see this huge body of water. Magellan believed that if he crossed this ocean he would reach the Spice Islands.

Vasco Núñez de Balboa

From Soldier to Sailor

Magellan was not always a sea captain. He had first served as a soldier. In 1505, he left for India, where Portugal battled to gain new lands. Magellan was a fearless soldier. More than once, he saved the lives of other Portuguese soldiers.

Around 1513, Magellan returned to Portugal. He then fought briefly in Morocco in northern Africa. He was seriously wounded there and walked with a limp for the rest of his life. Back in Portugal, Magellan decided to follow a dream. He wanted to lead an **expedition**

Magellan's coat of arms

to the Moluccas. His friend Francisco Serrão had been shipwrecked in the Moluccas and had decided to stay.

A village in the Moluccas as shown in a nineteenth century engraving

He sent Magellan letters describing the riches there.

King Manuel I, Portugal's king, was not interested in Magellan's plan, but Magellan refused to give up. He learned everything he could about **geography** and **navigation.** He studied maps and talked to sea captains. With that knowledge, Magellan headed for Spain.

In 1518, Magellan met with

King Manuel of Portugal

King Charles I of Spain. Magellan said he believed the Spice Islands belonged to Spain. Several years earlier, Spain and Portugal had signed a treaty splitting up land in the Americas and Asia. Most people believed the Spice Islands lay in the area claimed by Portugal. But Magellan thought the islands should actually belong to Spain. This argument helped convince Charles to support Magellan. The king and a wealthy businessman gave Magellan the money he needed for his expedition.

King Charles I of Spain

Magellan's Crew

Magellan was named captain-general for the trip. His ship was the *Trinidad.* The other ships in his fleet were the *San Antonio,*

The Victoria *as shown in a sixteenth century woodcut*

the *Concepción*, the *Victoria*, and the *Santiago*. The largest, the *San Antonio*, was probably about 70 feet (21.3 meters) long. (A modern cruise ship is easily ten times as long).

Magellan's crew came from many nations. One of the sailors was Henry, a slave Magellan had acquired during travels in Asia.

Some of the officers and other ship captains were Spanish political figures who had little experience at sea. To make things worse, they were not loyal to Magellan because he was Portuguese.

Another member of the crew was Antonio Pigafetta, an Italian nobleman who had volunteered to serve on the expedition. Pigafetta's diary offers the only complete report of the three-year trip around the world. In his first entries, Pigafetta calls Magellan "a wise and virtuous man and mindful of his honor."

A bust of Antonio Pigafetta

Setting Sail

Magellan's ships left Sanlucar de Barrameda, Spain, and headed for the Canary Islands. These islands lie in the Atlantic Ocean about 60 miles (97 kilometers) northwest of Africa. In the Canaries, Magellan received a letter warning him that the Spanish officers in his fleet planned to remove him as

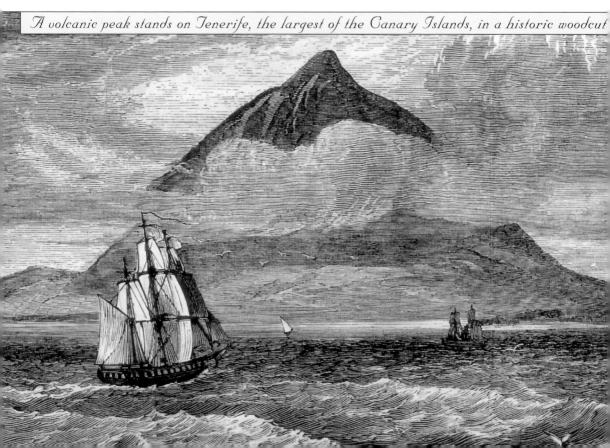

A volcanic peak stands on Tenerife, the largest of the Canary Islands, in a historic woodcut

The Canary Islands lie off the coast of Africa.

captain-general—and kill him if necessary. Magellan knew he had to be careful around his rivals.

Magellan left the Canaries on October 3 sailing south, close to the coast of Africa. Along the way, the ships ran into strong storms. Pigafetta wrote that the "wind and currents…came head-on to us so that we could not advance." The ships eventually got through the storms. As they neared the **equator,** they entered a part of the ocean called the **doldrums.** For days, the wind barely blew and the small fleet sat almost still in the water.

Life at sea was hard. Magellan had to cut back on the food and water each sailor could have, and heavy rains sometimes drenched the ships. Some of the

Spanish officers were angry that Magellan had set them on this course. He had discussed a different route back in Spain. Finally, one Spaniard could no longer control his hatred for Magellan.

An early map of the world omits the Americas.

During their time in the doldrums, the captain of the *Victoria* was accused of injuring a sailor. Magellan called all the other officers to his ship to hold a trial. Afterward, another captain,

---

An image from about 1520 shows Magellan and his ship.

Magellane nouo   te duce ducta freto.
Ambiui. meritoq̃   vocor VICTORIA: sunt mi
Vela, dlæ, preciū,   gloria, pugna, mare,

VICTORIA.

Conueniunt rebus nomina fepe suis.

Rio de Janeiro's harbor today

Juan de Cartagena, challenged Magellan's command. Magellan then grabbed Cartagena and placed him under arrest. Cartagena encouraged the other Spaniards to **mutiny,** or rebel, against Magellan. The officers refused however, and Cartagena remained under arrest.

The rest of the voyage across the Atlantic went smoothly, and Magellan's crew spotted land on December 8. The captain had reached his first goal—the coast of Brazil. A few days later he dropped anchor in the harbor of Rio de Janeiro. The first leg of the expedition was over.

Exploring South America

Magellan spent about two weeks repairing his ships and taking on more supplies. Then he sailed southward, looking for the strait that would lead to Balboa's unexplored ocean.

On January 11, 1520, the ships reached what is now Montevideo, the capital of Uruguay. Magellan sent the

The coast of Uruguay today

A group of Magellanic penguins on the Falkland Islands

Santiago to explore a passage he hoped was the strait. About two weeks later, the ship returned with bad news. The water passage was a huge river, not a strait. During the first week in February the fleet once again headed south, following the coast of present-day Argentina.

During the trip, Magellan and his crew saw animals unlike any they had ever seen. Pigafetta describes birds he called "geese." We know now that those birds were actually penguins. These birds and seals provided food for the crew.

South of the equator, the seasons are reversed from what they are in North America. During February in South America, autumn approached. Cool winds chilled the sailors, and then fierce storms battered the ships. Magellan searched for a spot where his fleet could spend the cold months. On March 31, he stopped at a harbor he named San Julian.

Mutiny

Trouble soon erupted at San Julian, however. The expedition's Spanish officers were still angry. They disliked the cold weather and the dangerous shoreline they were exploring. They still distrusted Magellan because he had changed the route. Now more of the officers talked of mutiny.

Leading this effort were Cartagena and Gaspar de Quesada, the captain of the *Concepción.* Cartagena was still under arrest, but Quesada released him so that they could carry out their mutiny.

On the night of April 1, Quesada, Cartagena, and several armed sailors took over the *San Antonio.* When an officer loyal to Magellan tried to stop the mutiny, Quesada said, "Must we be thwarted by this idiot?" and then stabbed the officer six times.

Magellan awoke the next morning to learn that three of his five ships were controlled by **mutineers.** He sent armed sailors to take back one of the ships. Once he had control of that vessel, Magellan blocked the harbor with his three ships.

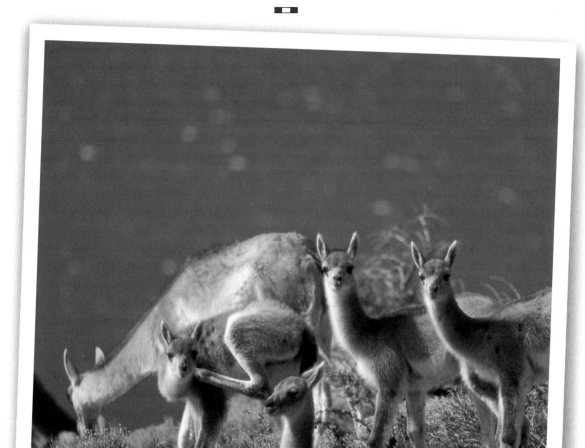

Guanacos, which are related to camels, live in South America.

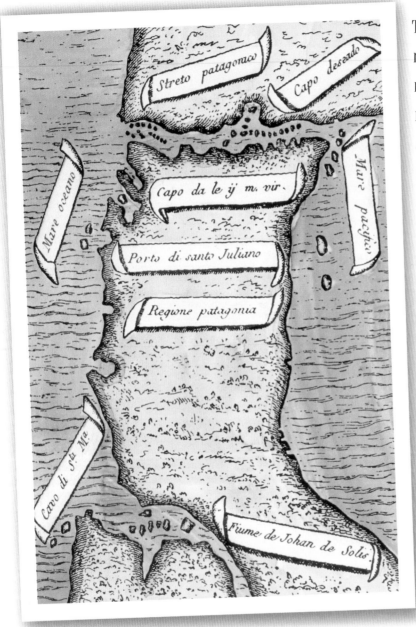

The remaining two rebel ships could not escape. The next day, Magellan and his crew regained control of the rebel ships. Quesada was killed; Cartagena and another mutineer were left on a small island. Magellan was in control once again.

This map appeared in an 1801 book about Pigafetta's trip with Magellan.

The Giants of Patagonia

During the winter, Magellan lost one of his ships—the *Santiago.* He had sent the *Santiago* to explore farther south but the ship ran aground during a storm. The crew walked 60 miles (96 km) to rejoin the fleet.

At San Julian, Magellan's crew met some native people. Pigafetta called them giants "so tall that the tallest of us only came up to [their] waist." These people were not actually giants, but they were apparently taller than most Europeans of the time.

The native people wore animal skins and

Magellan called the native people Patagonians.

A Tehuelche woman

painted their bodies. Today they are known as Tehuelches, but Magellan called them Patagonians. This name came from the Spanish word *pata,* meaning "paw," because the animal skins they wore as shoes made their feet look like paws. The part of South America where they lived is still called Patagonia.

A few of the "giants" became friendly with Magellan and his crew. They ate with the Europeans and accepted their gifts. Magellan decided to take some of the Patagonians back to Europe. He tricked two of them into putting on metal chains, and then took them on board his ship. However, neither of the Patagonians survived the trip back to Spain.

Magellan's Strait

In late August, Magellan left San Julian for a better winter port they would name Santa Cruz. There, the crew continued to repair the ships and find food.

Finally, on October 18, Magellan sailed again.

A few days later, Magellan's crew saw a large opening in the coastline. Magellan sent the two

Magellan discovers a strait to the west.

The Ona, shown in an 1895 photo, once lived on Tierra del Fuego.

in Uruguay. Magellan had at last discovered his strait to the west.

The ships sailed through the strait, exploring small bays along the way. Tall, snowcapped mountains rose behind steep cliffs near the water's edge. On the land to the south, natives burned fires through the night. This tip of South America still has the name Magellan gave it: *Tierra del Fuego,* meaning "Land of Fire."

About halfway through the strait, Magellan faced more trouble. Two men on the *San Antonio* took over the ship and headed back to Spain. However, Magellan had been sailing ahead in the strait, so

ships to explore it. They reported back with good news. This was not a river, as the fleet had found

Ships in the Strait of Magellan as shown in a nineteenth century engraving

An early map of the Strait of Magellan

many days passed before he learned that he had lost the ship. The *San Antonio* was the biggest ship in the fleet and carried most of the expedition's supplies. Magellan searched for the *San Antonio,* but eventually realized it was gone for good.

On November 21, Magellan asked all the remaining officers and high-ranking crew what they thought he should do. "Give me your opinion," Magellan wrote to them, "letting nothing prevent you from being entirely truthful." The crew knew what Magellan wanted to do, though. They continued the expedition.

A week later, the three ships sailed out of the strait, which today is called the Strait of Magellan. The ships entered the ocean Balboa had seen. The weather was good and the waters were smooth. Magellan called the ocean the *Pacific*, which means "calm" or "peaceful." He expected a short voyage across the ocean to the Spice Islands. Instead, he and his crew were beginning the longest and most difficult part of their journey.

The mountains of Tierra del Fuego today

Sailing in Unknown Waters

The three ships headed north, up the coast of what is now Chile. Around mid-December, they turned toward the northwest and the open waters of the Pacific. Before heading away

The Strait of Magellan today

from land, Magellan did not stop to take on more food. This was a costly mistake.

The journey across the Pacific went on for weeks. Magellan spotted several small islands along the way, but each time he decided it was too diffi-cult to anchor the ships and go ashore. Magellan also may have thought that the trip was almost over and he did not need to stop for food. Soon, **starvation** and disease spread throughout the ships.

Pigafetta describes how the crew "ate only old biscuits turned to powder, all full of worms and stinking." The men also ate ox hides, which they softened in the sea and then roasted over a flame. "And of

A map made soon after Magellan's discovery of the strait

the rats," Pigafetta says, "some of us could not get enough."

In early March, Magellan spotted another island, now known as Guam. Natives from the island greeted the fleet.

The beaches of Guam today

But when they boarded the ships and began taking the sailors' possessions, the crew chased the natives away. The next day, Magellan sent armed men ashore to attack the natives, whom he considered thieves. The crew burned the natives' homes and killed seven villagers. Then they gathered fresh fruit for themselves and filled barrels with water. Despite the attack, the Guamanians were not afraid of Magellan's men. A few came out to trade more food for some of the items on the ships.

The Philippines

After leaving Guam, Magellan sailed west. About a week later, he spotted Samar, one of the islands in the chain now called the Philippines. Once again, native people rowed out to greet the ships. This time, Magellan offered them cloth, combs, and mirrors in exchange for food and water.

A village beneath Mount Mayon in the Philippines as shown in a nineteenth century engraving

On March 28, Magellan heard something wonderful. His slave, Henry, called to the natives in Malay and the natives responded in the same language! Magellan realized he was near the Spice Islands, because Malay was spoken throughout that part of the world. Magellan and his men had become the first Europeans to sail west and reach Asia.

Magellan took on more food for his ships. He and his crew also attended festivals with the native people. In early April, Magellan headed for Cebu, the main trading center of the region. There he signed a peace treaty with Humabon, the island's ruler. Magellan also convinced Humabon to become a Christian. Most European explorers of the era tried to spread their religion in new lands. More than 2,000 people on Cebu and nearby islands eventually became Christians.

Magellan's preserved wooden cross is on display in Cebu beneath a ceiling painting that depicts his landing.

The Last Battle

Magellan thought Cebu could be an important port for Spain so he demanded that the neighboring chiefs recognize Humabon as their leader. When one chief refused, Magellan sent men to attack his village.

A chief called Lapulapu also refused to obey Magellan and dared the Europeans to attack his village. Magellan was sure he could defeat Lapulapu and his men. He planned an attack on the island of Mactan, which was ruled by Lapulapu. Humabon provided 1,000 warriors to help Magellan fight. He offered to have his troops go first. But Magellan insisted that his crew would lead the assault.

On the morning of April 27, Magellan led forty-nine soldiers

Magellan's ships attack Mactan.

ashore at Mactan. However, they were far outnumbered by Lapulapu's men. Arrows, spears, and stones rained down upon the Europeans in the bloody battle that followed.

Magellan died in a bloody battle.

Magellan fought bravely. Wounded several times, he finally fell face down on the ground. A group of warriors then attacked Magellan with spears, killing him.

Magellan's death on April 27, 1521, is shown in a nineteenth century engraving.

The Journey Home

Magellan's death stunned many of the crew but they knew they had to go on. First, they burned the *Concepción*, since they did not have enough sailors now for three ships.

Only the Victoria *made it back to Spain.*

The remaining two ships sailed west. The *Trinidad* and the *Victoria* finally reached the Spice Islands in November 1521. Only the *Victoria* left for Spain, however. The *Trinidad* stayed behind for repairs.

Ferdinand Magellan

The *Victoria* sailed across the Indian Ocean and around Africa. On September 6, 1522, the ship finally made it home to Spain. The world's first circumnavigation was over.

The survivors gave different versions of their trip. Pigafetta's diary praised Magellan, but the captain of the *Victoria* blamed Magellan for the mutiny and for losing the battle at Mactan. Spaniards in general refused to give Magellan much credit for his historic voyage because he was Portuguese. For many years, some Portuguese considered him a traitor to his own country because he had sailed for Spain.

Today, most people realize the importance of Magellan's journey. He pursued the bold idea that he could sail west and reach Asia. He led his crew on a long and dangerous voyage. And his journey made clear the true size of oceans and of the entire globe. "No other," Pigafetta said of Magellan, "had so much natural wit, boldness, or knowledge to sail once around the world."

A monument to Magellan stands in Punta Arenas, Chile.

Glossary

circumnavigation—going around the Earth by water

destination—the place to which one is traveling

doldrums—a calm part of the ocean near the equator; a slump

equator—an imaginary line around the Earth

expedition—a journey taken to find, learn, or acquire something

geography—the study of the Earth's surface, and its land and water features

investigate—study; examine carefully

mutineer—someone who takes part in a mutiny

mutiny—a rebellion by a ship's crew against the captain

navigation—the science of getting a ship from place to place

nobility—the ruling class

privilege—a special right or advantage

starvation—suffering or dying from lack of food

strait—a narrow waterway connecting two large bodies of water

Did You Know?

- Magellan's voyage proved without question that Earth is a sphere.

- Magellan's voyage proved that Earth's oceans are connected.

- Food was so scarce on the voyage that Magellan's crew even ate sawdust.

- A presidential railcar named The Ferdinand Magellan is now a national historic landmark. It is on display at the Gold Coast Railroad Museum in Miami, Florida.

- Magellan and his crew used sand clocks (hourglasses) to tell time onboard ship.

- In 1989, the United States launched a spacecraft named *Magellan* to map the surface of Venus.

Important Dates in Magellan's Life

1480
Magellan born in north-west Portugal

1513
Returns to Portugal; is wounded during a battle in Morocco

1505
Leaves for India

1517
Arrives in Spain

1518
Receives support from King Charles I for an expedition to the Spice Islands

1519
Leaves Spain, sailing west toward the New World

1520
Sails through the Strait of Magellan and reaches the Pacific Ocean

1521
Dies on April 21 in the Philippines

1522
One of Magellan's original five ships returns to Spain

Important People

CARTAGENA, JUAN DE (?) captain of the *San Antonio* who planned a mutiny against Magellan

CHARLES I (1500–1558) king of Spain 1516–1556 also known as Charles V, Holy Roman Emperor 1519–1556

COLUMBUS, CHRISTOPHER (1451–1506) an Italian explorer, convinced King Ferdinand and Queen Isabella of Spain to finance his attempt to reach Asia by sailing west

HUMABON (?) ruler of the island of Cebu

LAPULAPU (?) ruler of the island of Mactan where Magellan was killed

MAGELLAN, FERDINAND (1480–1521) Portuguese navigator who led the expedition that resulted in the first circumnavigation of the globe

MANUEL I (1469–1521) king of Portugal from 1495–1521

NÚÑEZ DE BALBOA, VASCO (1475–1519) Spanish explorer and first European in the Americas to see the Pacific Ocean

PIGAFETTA, ANTONIO (1491–(?)1534) one of the eighteen survivors of Magellan's crew. He later wrote an account of the trip for the king

QUESADA, GASPAR DE (?–1520) captain of the *Concepción* who planned a mutiny along with Cartagena

SERRÃO, FRANCISCO (?) friend of Magellan's who was shipwrecked in the Moluccas and wrote him letters describing the riches to be found there

Want to Know More?

At the Library

Fritz, Jean. *Around the World in a Hundred Years: From Henry the Navigator to Magellan.* New York: Putnam, 1994.

Gallagher, Jim. *Ferdinand Magellan and the First Voyage Around the World.* Philadelphia: Chelsea House, 2000.

Ganeri, Anita. *Ferdinand Magellan.* Mankato, Minn.: Thameside Press, 1999.

Jacobs, William Jay. *Magellan: Voyager With a Dream.* New York: Franklin Watts, 1994.

Mattern, Joanne, and Patrick O'Brien (illustrator). *The Travels of Ferdinand Magellan.* Austin, Tex.: Raintree Steck-Vaugh, 2000.

Stefoff, Rebecca. *Ferdinand Magellan and the Discovery of the World Ocean.* Broomall, Penn.: Chelsea House, 1990.

On the Web

For more information on *Ferdinand Magellan,* use FactHound to track down Web sites related to this book.

1. Go to *www.facthound.com*
2. Type in a search word related to this book or this book ID: 0756501253
3. Click on the *Fetch It* button.

Your trusty FactHound will fetch the best Web sites for you!

Through the Mail

Philippines Department of Tourism
T.M. Kalaw Street
Rizal Park
P.O. Box 3451
Manila, Philippines
For information about the island group Magellan
visited and the place where he met his death

On the Road

The Mariners' Museum
100 Museum Drive
Newport News, VA 23606
757/596-2222
To see exhibits about navigators and sailors

Index

About the Author

Michael Burgan is a freelance writer for children and adults. A history graduate of the University of Connecticut, he has written more than thirty fiction and nonfiction children's books for various publishers. For adult audiences, he has written news articles, essays, and plays. Michael Burgan is a recipient of an Edpress Award and belongs to the Society of Children's Book Writers and Illustrators.